You Are Destined For GREATNESS

21 DAY DEVOTIONAL FOR THE BROKEN HEARTED

KALIE KLETT

Copyright © 2020 Kalie Klett

All rights reserved.

Anointed Words Publishing Company

ISBN:
978-1-947558-42-7

DEDICATION

I dedicate this book to God; I thank God for all that he's brought me through and all he will continue to bring me through. I'm also thankful for all the inspiration God has blessed me within this season.

I also dedicate this book to everything and everyone the enemy tried to use against me. For that I will forever have a testimony to use for the glory of God.

ACKNOWLEDGMENTS

I would most importantly like to thank my Pastors Michael and Kim Lyons of In Faith Ministries for always believing in me and pouring into me. I am so thankful for the way they encourage me daily, the way they push me, and the way they love as Christ loves. I love you both and appreciate you more than words!

I would also like to thank Pastor Marti Landis of City Harvest Ministries; God has used her tremendously in my walk with Christ. She has continuously encouraged and pushed me into the purpose God has for my life. I am very thankful for you!

I would like to acknowledge Dr. Leah McCray, of Anointed Words Publishing, for her patience, help, and encouragement during the process of writing and publishing this book. Thank you!

Contents

DEDICATION 1

ACKNOWLEDGMENTS 2

INTRODUCTION 6

THOUGHTS FROM THE ENEMY 8

EMOTIONS ARE DECIETFUL 11

TRAUMATIC DREAMS 14

DEALING WITH YOUR ISSUES 18

THE SPIRIT OF DEPRESSION 21

RAPE 25

SUICIDE ATTEMPT 29

SEPERATION OF PARENTS 34

NIGHTLY PANIC ATTACKS 39

PHYSICAL ABUSE 45

SOUL TIE 50

FIGHTING THE DARKNESS 55

LOOSING A FRIENDSHIP 59

DREAMS FROM GOD VS. DREAMS FROM THE DEVIL 63

YOUR AGE DOESN'T DEFINE HOW GOD WILL USE YOU 67

DEMONIC SPIRITS 72

STEPPING OUT IN FAITH 76

BOLDNESS 80

SPIRITUAL RELATIONSHIPS 83

UNANSWERED PRAYERS	86
YOU ARE QUALIFIED	89
ABOUT THE AUTHOR	92

INTRODUCTION

Everyone wants healed but never wants to put the work in. It's very critical to put the work required in when you desire to be healed.

See I never knew I had to work my healing out; that was until I had an encounter with God, and he told me this thing is real…. Not everything is freely given, there are somethings you have to work for.

In you are destined for GREATNESS, I share different parts of my testimony. I've chosen to share times that I have been most vulnerable with the intention of helping you walk out your healing.

I believe as you continue to walk out your healing day by day you will be healed, set free, and delivered from the pain you've been holding onto for years.

It's time to be healed!

THOUGHTS FROM THE ENEMY

2 Corinthians 10:5

"Casting down imaginations, and every high thing that exalteth itself against the knowledge of God and bringing into captivity every thought to the obedience of Christ."

You will never be loved, you're ugly, go kill yourself, your family hates you, you will never be healed. Do you hear and have these thoughts daily? Because I used to... But God!!

You must get to the place where you KNOW you are so much more. When these thoughts start to pop up you have to be able to bind them up and cast them down (2 Corinthians 10:5). When you get to the spot where you are casting those thoughts down you are walking in the holy spirit and not the devil spirit.

All my childhood, I walked with the devil spirit before I realized that there was a holy spirit. It's time to rise up as Christians and worship the one and only real God. When you have God within you, NOTHING is impossible.

God will remind you daily that you have always been loved (John 3:16), You were wonderfully and fearfully made in His image (Psalm 139:14), You Have so much value (Genesis 1:27), You will be healed (Psalm 147:2).

You have got to get to the spot where you have bound up that devil spirit and cast it down and you are now walking with the Holy Spirit. When the holy spirit is within you, you need to start walking this thing out. You need to start to walk in the purpose God has for you (Jeremiah 29:11) He has great plans for your life. Walk-in it. You are loved!

Daily Declarations:

- **I am more than enough!**
- **I declare Not only will I, but my family will also walk with the Holy Spirit!**
- **I command the devil spirit to be gone!**

EMOTIONS ARE DECIETFUL

Proverbs 3:5-6

"Trust in and rely confidently on the Lord with all your heart and do not rely on your own insight or understanding. In all your ways know and acknowledge and recognize him, and he will make your paths straight and smooth [removing obstacles that block your way]."

Do you let your emotions control your life? To the point that you hate your life because you're always depressed, sad, frustrated, and never happy?

Come on now, let us be honest we all have been to the point where we let our emotions control us. However, our emotions are deceitful, they lie to us and make us think things are way worse than they really are.

In Proverbs 3:5-6 God says do not rely on your understanding but in all you do, rely on him. He says that because he knows how deceitful our emotions really are.

He knows how the enemy will use our emotions to tempt us into things, not of God and pull us right into sin. But when we rely on God and not our emotions the enemy has absolutely no control over our lives. When the enemy knows he has no control over our lives he will try to attack but he will *Never* win for we already have the victory.

So tonight, give your emotions to God! Deal with them and watch how you grow!

Daily Declarations:

- ➤ I will rely on God and Not my own Understand!
- ➤ I bind up all attacks against the enemy and declare he will stay under my feet!
- ➤ I already have the victory!

TRAUMATIC DREAMS

Luke 10:19

"Look, I have given you authority over all the power of the enemy, and you can walk among snakes and scorpions and crush them. Nothing will injure you."

It's time to get ready for a good night's rest but you don't want to close your eyes because of the dreams you've been having. The enemy keeps showing up and playing the one night you never wanted to remember; that night you were traumatized from the amount of hurt done to your life. He started showing up in your dreams with the boy you thought you'd marry but the enemy just used him to scar you deeper.

Now you find yourself fighting your sleep every night because you know the enemy is going to attack you again and the pain is just too much to bear. You are at the point where you are just so tired of being awakened out of your sleep, in full-blown tears and panic attacks.

You keep telling yourself this is your fault, and this is what you deserve BUT you are very wrong! God created you for so much more. You have all Authority over every single one of those dreams.

I encourage you to start to speak declarations over those dreams. (ex: I release the power and authority of the Lord against all demons I encounter. Lord, cause the powers of darkness to submit to your powers. I declare I will lay my head down and no spirit of the enemy will even be able to enter my mind in the name of Jesus.

If you still wake up after speaking these declarations, then get out of bed and start walking around your room and speaking in your heavenly language. (The enemy is threatened by your spiritual language because he cannot understand it.) Then speak your declarations again and go back to bed. Once you start to do these things the enemy will leave you alone; maybe not immediately, but it will happen.

Daily Devotional:

- In the name of Jesus, I command these dreams not of God to be gone.
- I have all authority over these attacks and declare they will stop right now in the mighty name of Jesus!
- I speak peace over my room, my mind, and my dreams in the name of Jesus!

DEALING WITH YOUR ISSUES

Psalm 30:5

"For his anger is but for a moment, His favor is for a lifetime. Weeping may endure for a night, but a shout of joy comes in the morning."

At certain points in our lives, we have certain things that pop up, things that have scarred us deep down on the inside. These things are usually issues that we have buried deep within us and decided to tuck away and ignore.

Burying those issues deep within hinders you from all God has for you. I know right now it feels as if those issues have wounded you so deep and that the scar left behind will never heal, but believe me, I was there, and God took an issue I had buried for 7 years and started to heal it. That doesn't mean it didn't take time but, day by day, it does get better and better.

That's what God wants for you, once you get to the place that you deal with those emotions, God will use those very issues you HAD for his glory! Once you start to testify, those issues will be used for God's glory and not only will they be used BUT you will be blessed.

God loves the fact you were obedient and dealt with those things that made you uncomfortable. He loves the fact that you trust and love him so much you gave him those things that cut you deep, deep down on the inside. Those issues that had you up for nights crying out to the Lord, will soon be the very things that bring joy not only to you and the Lord but also to the people you speak life into with your testimony!!

You are the light. Don't give up; someone needs to hear your story!

Today's Declarations:

- ➢ **I will be healed and delivered in the mighty name of Jesus!**
- ➢ **Lord I give you all of me, father, use me for your glory!**
- ➢ **I declare that my testimony would be used to minister to millions in the name of Jesus!**

THE SPIRIT OF DEPRESSION

Psalm 40:1-2

"I waited patiently and expectantly for the Lord; he inclined me and heard my cry. He brought me up out of a horrible pit, out of the miry clay, And He set my feet upon a rock, steadying my footsteps and establishing my path."

Anxiety, tears, anger, loneliness, sadness, and Insomnia or extreme tiredness…. If you're a doctor you would tell me these are all signs of depression. A doctor would also tell you the only treatment is counseling and anti-depressants.

I know, I've been there. I remember lying awake at night asking myself why I wasn't enough, why everyone hated me, why all these things were happening to me.

I remember having to fight myself to get out of bed daily. I started to see no point in any of it. I started to feel useless more and more each day. But one day I remember crying out to God and hearing him tell me, "Daughter I've never left your side I've always been right here."

I want to tell you what I was never told during my hard time. You are worth so much more than you could ever imagine, you have a purpose, you have a destiny, and God placed you on this earth for a reason, he breathed his breath in you because you have a purpose.

That "disease" the doctors call

depression is just an attack from the enemy and all you have to do is declare that you will be delivered from the spirit of depression and watch God work.

He is a way maker, he is a healer, he will deliver to you! Truly believe it in your heart and watch God work. God hears every single one of your cries. Right now, you are in a season of reaping but once you move into a season of harvest every single one of those tears you cried will be doubled and the blessings will be bigger than ever imaginable.

Today's Declarations:

- I declare right now in the mighty name of Jesus that the spirit of depression would bow down in the name of Jesus
- I break every single generation curse of depression right now in the name of Jesus
- I declare that no spirit coming against me will prosper in the mighty name of Jesus

RAPE

Romans 12:17-18

"Never repay anyone evil for evil. Take thought for what is right and gracious and proper in the sight of everyone. If possible, as far as it depends on you, live at peace with everyone."

You're running around outside on a beautiful sunny summer day with no cares and worries in the world. That was until the most valuable thing was taken from you... your virginity without consent.

You remember being a child laying in the bed feeling so hopeless and weak, you remember the pain you felt as that person took your clothes off and took complete advantage of you. After that night you felt useless, you felt a pain you've never experienced before, that night your heart was broken in a way you never knew it could break.

You have had many sleepless nights. You've had dreams of that day being replayed. You've had days you could feel the pain as if it was happening all over again.

These are all normal for rape victims, this can be a very hard and vulnerable topic, but it has to be addressed as there are so many women and men who have never talked about it because of the shame and guilt they feel from it.

God sees all that pain you feel each

night, he sees the way the enemy is coming up against you, he hears the prayers of other people but is waiting to hear from you.

He wants to hear you cry out so that he can touch your heart in a way you never knew possible. He also wants you to forgive the person who hurt you, but you can't do that until God starts to heal you.

These are all very critical steps in the healing process. Remember Pain comes in the night, but joy comes in the morning. When the pain starts to show up, remember who you are. You are more than the Woman/Man that got raped.

You are a conquer, you are victorious, you are the Head and not the tail, you are the child of a King. Keep Pressing and moving into your healing.

Today's Declaration:

- **I can see my healing, I can feel my deliverance, it is coming in the name of Jesus**
- **I plead the blood of Jesus over my mind, heart, and soul and command Satan to flee right now in the name of Jesus**
- **I speak peace over my life right now in the name of Jesus**

SUICIDE ATTEMPT

James 4:7

"Therefore, submit to God. Resist the devil and his lies, and he will flee from you."

One cut, two cuts, three cuts, four and before you know it you've got tons of blood running down your arm. You told yourself just one more cut will take the pain away, it will numb the pain, it will take the memories of the pain away.

The next day comes and you find yourself hearing voices in your head telling you how worthless you are, how no one loves you, and to take your life already. That last voice hurt you deep down... you keep hearing it on repeat. Go kill yourself,

Go kill yourself, Go kill yourself. You start to hear those three words daily.

One day you go to school and it's the worst day ever. Your "best friend" gets mad at you and tells you to go kill yourself. That completely tore you apart. You run straight home, run up to the bathroom, grab those pills you've been fighting against and a pack of razor blades.

You start the shower get undressed and sit in the bathtub. As you are sitting in the bath, you grab the razor blades and start cutting your wrist and, as you're cutting your wrist, you try to cut deeper than ever before.

You realize the pain isn't going away, so as the bathtub is filling up with your blood, dripping from your wrist, you grab that bottle of pills and take all 30.

Your mom walks in and instantly falls to her knees when she sees your lifeless body lying there. She doesn't know what else to do so she prays... She promises God that if he doesn't take her baby, she will praise and worship him always.

As You are getting rushed to the hospital. Your mom prays for the first time ever. When the doctors come out, they tell your mom things don't look good for you. They do all they can, but it wasn't enough, they tell your mom you didn't make it, that was until God decided you still had a purpose on earth. When your mom walks in blaming herself, your heart starts to beat again, and you gain consciousness.

God woke you up again because you have a destiny, he has a plan for you. He has a plan to prosper and not harm you. His plan is for good and not evil. When those voices start to pop up in your head plead the blood of Jesus and rebuke those voices and start speaking the word of God.

When we stand firm on the word of God the devil will flee. The devil has already lost the battle and you already have the victory!!

Today's Declaration:

- I Command the spirit of depression to flee far away from me in the Name of Jesus!
- I speak victory over my life, I am victorious, and will move forward as a victorious child of God!
- I plead the blood of Jesus over the spirit of suicide and command it to bow down to the name of Jesus!

SEPERATION OF PARENTS

Deuteronomy 31:8

"The Lord himself goes before you and will be with you; he will never leave you nor forsake you. Do not be afraid; do not be discouraged."

One day you're an infant and you have both your parents by your side and in a blink of an eye one of them just up and left you. They left you with so much more than hurt. They left you with trust issues, a broken heart, and anger aimed at the world.

You are the oldest out of all your siblings and the parent who stayed to take care of you is so broken they can barely support you and your siblings. So, with you being the oldest sibling, you're forced to grow up and play that parent role.

You don't know how or what it looks like, but you know you have to pick it up. It isn't easy picking that role up, but you start to grow into a routine with it. You grow apart from your childhood because you are busy helping support your family... working two jobs in high school, maintaining good grades, and dealing with all the household work on top of schoolwork.

As you grow older you truly realize how your parent's absence has really affected you. You find yourself staying awake at night asking yourself regularly why you weren't enough for that parent and what did I do wrong. You start to realize the heaviness of the weight you have been carrying for years and start to realize how worthless you feel.

You feel so worthless and have learned to distance yourself. Your mind tells you if your parent could leave you so would everyone else. You don't know how to cope with the pain because you are supposed to be the "strong" one, but it just hurts.

I'm here to tell you that it is okay to cry out. I don't know what you've been told but tears ARE NOT a sign of weakness they are a sign of strength. Once you let the hurt out you grow in a way you never would have imagined. When we keep the hurt in it hinders us and keeps us in bondage... away from the things God has for us.

I also want to let you know you NEVER have to distance yourself from God. He isn't like our natural parents. He is OUR father that told us in his word that he would NEVER leave nor forsake us. He isn't a God that can lie.

It can be hard at first to trust him but when you get into the word and start to strengthen your relationship with him, trusting him becomes extremely easy. God always shows his word to be true. If you are someone holding back from God because of a parent leaving I encourage you to get into the word and grow a closer relationship with God; he will not disappoint you!

Today's Declaration:

- I break off the generational curse of broken families over myself and my siblings right now in the name of Jesus!
- I will put all my trust into God my father!
- I speak peace and Joy over my life in the mighty name of Jesus!

NIGHTLY PANIC ATTACKS

Isaiah 43:2

"When you pass through the waters, I will be with you; and when you pass through the rivers, they won't sweep over you. When you walk through the fire, you won't be scorched, and the flame won't burn you.

It's 4 A.M and you suddenly wake up out of your sleep. When you open your eyes you can barely breath; you're panting for air, your arms are shaking as if you haven't eaten in days, your mouth feels as if it's swollen shut, and you have an endless amount of drool coming out of your mouth.

This isn't the first night this has happened. This has been happening for over two weeks along with the enemy attacking your mind. However, this night was different because when you woke up you noticed a burning on your upper thigh but couldn't see anything, so you turned on the light.

When you turned on the light, you noticed a rash and tons of scratches. The majority of your thigh was covered in scratches. At first none of it made sense until you started to think about it. You remember the way the enemy had been attacking your dreams and you also remember that each time you have those dreams you wake up in a full-blown panic attack.

You start to pray and then God reveals that... this is all the enemies doing.

As you process what God told you, you start to question God, like why wouldn't you protect me? I've been faithful and obedient, and you let this happen? What did I do wrong? Why, God, why?

God answers you back, Child you've been questioning your strength recently; you've been telling yourself how weak you are but this needed to happen so I could prove to you just how strong you really are. I told you I wouldn't allow something to happen to you that you can't handle. You needed this to happen so you could see just how strong you really are. Remember no weapon formed against you shall prosper. The next time you wake up in a panic attack like this I want you to fight, fight like you've never fought before. Completely trust me and watch me remove it in a blink of an eye.

Sometimes God does things just to show us that those thoughts we have going on in our head are wrong, sometimes God tests our faith, and sometimes God does things because he's God. Regardless of the reasoning, God won't let the enemy put something on us that would take us out.

In the scripture above he says that through all the storms he will be with us and that none of it would be able to burn us. We have to get to the place as the body of Christ where we stop questioning God and just trust him. When we truly trust and have faith in a person, we don't question them so stop questioning God.

If this is you, I encourage you to

surrender and completely put your trust in God, Keep praying, and keep speaking in your heavenly language. The devil will flee; it just takes time!

Today's Declaration:

- ➤ Father I surrender every piece of me that I have closed off from you and as of right now I give you complete access.
- ➤ Right now, I come against any and all Spirits of panic I command them to flee from my body right now in the name of Jesus!
- ➤ Lord right now I speak with my mouth and declare that I will put all of my trust in you. When I don't

understand I will put my trust in you, when it makes no sense, I'll put my trust in you, and when the enemy attacks I will put my trust in you!

PHYSICAL ABUSE

Psalms 147:3

"God heals the brokenhearted and bandages their wounds."

You meet one of the most charming, caring, and loving men. A man who loves you like you've never been loved. You feel like you are in the best relationship ever, or at least you thought.

Your relationship starts out amazing and after a few months go by, things start to go downhill. They go downhill in a way you never even imagined. You will never forget the first time he laid a hand on you.

You are both in the kitchen laughing and the next thing you know, you say something that upsets him, and he slaps you right across the face.

You are in more shock at the time then you are in pain. You convince yourself that this was a one-time thing and that it was an accident and he did it out of love, but it was only the beginning of this journey.

Having hands laid on you starts to be the norm; it continues to happen at least once, if not more than twice a day. You start to tell yourself he's only doing this because he loves you but deep down on the inside, you know the only reason you are staying is due to fear.

You are scared if you leave, he will find you and hurt you worse. You're scared of what others will think. You're scared of the change. As months go on, you start to develop many bruises all over your body and you tell your parents it's because you are super clumsy. So, they think nothing of it.

After it seems like you have no other option, you go to your last resort and start praying and actually getting into God's word. When you start reading you learn that God said the enemy was out to kill, steal, and destroy and he was for death but God, he is so much more, he is life. He is a healer, he is a miracle worker, he heals the brokenhearted.

So, one day you drop to your knees and beg God to take you far away from this relationship and to never allow this man to hurt you again. After you pray, the next day while he is at work you pack your belongings and leave. You move back in with your family who live hours away. You never heard from him again, you start to thank God. You realize his word is true, he truly is a way maker, a miracle worker, and a light in the darkness! He is life! He took me out of a 9-month abusive relationship and will do the same for you!

If you have ever been or are currently in an abusive relationship, I just encourage you to lean on God word. God has so much better for you. God never intended for any of that to happen, but God wants you to know that there is a way out of it. You just have to trust in the Lord and believe him when he says no weapon formed against you shall prosper! He has amazing plans for your life and this testimony you now have is one of them!!

Today's Declaration:

- **I declare that no weapon formed against me shall prosper in the mighty name of Jesus!!**
- **I rebuke the spirit of death right now and speak the spirit of life into my life in the name of Jesus!!**
- **I command the spirit of abuse to flee far far far from my life and declare that I will no longer live in fear!!!**

SOUL TIE

James 2:19

"You say you have faith, for you believe that there is one God. Good for you! Even the demons believe this, and they tremble in terror."

Have you ever talked to someone for a short amount of time? Maybe even a long amount of time and roots were attached deep down inside of you. A soul tie was formed.

Did you feel as if you were never going to be able to get past those feelings? Like that person was supposed to be your forever? Now God separated that relationship and your emotions have gotten the best of you.

Not only have your emotions got the best of you but now the enemy sees how vulnerable you are and has decided since he can't get to you any other way, he's going to show up in your dreams.

He knows he can reach you through your dreams. So, the first night he shows up in a subtle way. All you do is hear your ex's voice and It hurts but not as bad as the other nights. After a few nights pass the enemy goes from a subtle way to full-on tormenting you.

He changes the dream from just a voice, to harm being done to you in those dreams. You wake up wondering if it would ever get better and thinking there is no way it could get worse; that is, until the next night you wake up from those dreams again and you remember a burning on your thigh. You couldn't see anything, so you turn on your light and notice your thighs are completely covered in scratches from your thigh to your knee. It was then you realized the attack by the enemy was real.

You don't know what else to do but call on the name Jesus. You know that demons tremble at the name of Jesus and you know there is power in the name of Jesus, so you just start calling him name. Jesus! Jesus! Jesus! There is so much power in his name.

The enemy may think he's got you, but he is so wrong. You call on the name of Jesus and you watch as the whole thing flips.

Demons tremble at the name of Jesus. The enemy has no power over the name of Jesus. Jesus took all the power from him when he was nailed to the cross.

If you are dealing with a situation like this or any kind of situation where you are being attacked by the enemy just start calling on the name of Jesus. God will intervene and turn this whole thing around for your good!

Today's Declaration:

- I Plead the blood of Jesus over my body, soul, and mind.
- I command all Demonic spirits coming up against my mind to tremble to the name of Jesus
- I declare that there is power in the name of Jesus, there is life in his name, and I shall live and not die.

FIGHTING THE DARKNESS
Joshua 1:5

"I will never leave nor forsake you."

To you it's just another miserable day. A day that consists of you fighting your mind. On the outside you look so happy but, on the inside, you are fighting a battle. A very dark battle. A battle darker than anyone would ever think you were battling.

Every weekday you get up you go to school, and during lunch you sit by yourself, then when you go home you sit in your room by yourself, and at dinner your family doesn't talk to you.

These things have all caused you to

isolate yourself from other people. You feel like you don't fit in, like you will never fit in and you will never lose this feeling of being lonely.

As you get older you choose to isolate yourself from people because you have never felt like you belong. This isolation causes the devil to mess with your mind. He tells you daily no one likes you and no one will ever like you. It will always be JUST you, never anyone else. You will live this life alone and you will die alone. You hear this in your head daily.

Every day you start to isolate yourself more and more until it's to the point you only leave your house when you have to. Other then that, you stay to yourself in your bedroom. You don't interact with others; you just lay in bed and wonder why you have such darkness on the inside, but you have no answers.

I'm here to tell you the answer is Jesus! He will take that darkness away in a blink of an eye. He tells us, in his word, that he would never leave nor forsake us, meaning you are NEVER alone, and you NEVER have to isolate yourself.

God will link you with the right people. People who won't single you out, people who will love you unconditionally, and people who will never let you feel alone.

I encourage you that if you haven't accepted Jesus in your heart to accept him and watch change start to happen within you. Remember you are NEVER alone. God is always there and always listening!

Today's Declaration:

- ➢ **I am NEVER alone for my God is with me today and every day.**
- ➢ **I have a purpose one which doesn't include loneliness but one that includes fellowship.**
- ➢ **I speak death to the spirit of loneliness in the mighty name of Jesus!**

LOOSING A FRIENDSHIP

Daniel 2:21

"It is he who changes the times and seasons; He removes kings and establishes kings. He gives wisdom to the wise and greater knowledge to those who have understanding!"

We all have that one friend we pray we never lose, that person that you are with 24/7, that person you can't imagine not being in your life. I had one of those too.

I literally was so dependent on her. We did basically everything together. We were literally always together; we even took our first vacation together; little did I know that it would be our last.

Shortly after that, God revealed to me that this person wasn't healthy and in fact, they were hindering my growth with him for a few reasons. Number one, I was so dependent on this person and not myself. Reason 2, this person was so negative, and it started to rub off on me.

So, at that point, God separated me from that person. He completely removed our relationship. At first, I was so lost I didn't know what to do. I found myself fighting myself to go to church because I didn't want to be uncomfortable, but God still got me to go and the most amazing things started to happen when he separated that relationship... I started to grow for real!

I began to grow a real personal relationship with God, I was connected with other people at church, I was at my happiest point in life. At that point I realized separation causes Elevation!!!

Sometimes God makes us uncomfortable because if he didn't, we would have never moved. I guarantee if God would have forced our friendship to end, I would never have been bold enough to end it myself.

God has a plan behind all he does. We may not understand it but that's okay because he is God and he knows what he has planned. Trust God! The process behind it is beautiful. A process to connect you with others, a plan for your growth, a plan to prosper you! His plan is more than you could ever imagine.

Today's Declaration:

- **Lord reveal those relationship to us that need to be separated**
- **I declare the separation from these friendships will elevate me!**
- **I speak death to any and all friendships hinder my growth**

DREAMS FROM GOD VS. DREAMS FROM THE DEVIL
Joel 2:28

"It shall come to pass afterwards, that I will pour out my spirit upon everyone; Your sons and daughters will prophesy, your old men will dream dreams, and your young men will see visions."

Does God talk to you through your dreams? Or do you at least think he tries to? Me too! God talks to me all of the time through my dreams. However, with God speaking through our dreams also comes the enemy.

The devil comes in so many different

ways. Sometimes we'll have a dream and truly think it was sent straight from God and not even pray about it and that's our mistake. We need to pray and confirm it is a dream from God before we take the step into fulfilling whatever they dream may have been.

Sometimes the enemy will also torment us in our dreams... there are a few reasons. Reason number one, he knows how close we are to fulfilling the purpose and destiny God has for us and that scares him. Reason number 2, he wants us to get distracted and off track, so we don't hear the dream and vision God has for us. And reason number 3, he is out to torment us (he wants to kill, steal, and destroy).

This is why it is so critical to pray and ask God; was that you God? What does this mean? What is next? Always make sure you confirm your dreams with God. Also, always write them down. If you are a dreamer on a normal basis keep a journal/notebook beside your bed and when you wake from that dream write it down, so you don't forget. These dreams are critical to walking into the full purpose and destiny has for you!

Daily Declaration:

- ➢ **I will not allow the enemy to throw me off track**
- ➢ **I will be obedient to all God shows reveals to me in my dreams**

- I will walk in my purpose and destiny; I will not question my ability… I am equipped

YOUR AGE DOESN'T DEFINE HOW GOD WILL USE YOU
Romans 2:11

"For God does not show favoritism."

Are you a younger woman of God? A woman who has put her whole life and passion in the Lord? Not because you want to draw attention but simply because you love the Lord.

Do you just want to be obedient and really live this thing out? Have you had someone try to tell you that you don't really hear God and you're too young to have a purpose or calling?

Let me tell you, that's the devil speaking!! I'm currently 19 years old, pursuing God and the purpose he has for me each and every day. I've shared my testimony in front of a group of people, I'm writing a book, I'm a leader over a ministry, and mentoring multiple young girls.

I tell you this because I'm young and being used in so many ways, so don't EVER let someone tell you that you are too young. I've had many people try to speak death over me; they've tried to get me distracted and off track. The devil will use those people to get you off track for he knows the mighty plans God has for you at such a young age!

Listen to me, it is rare today to have such young ladies fully pursuing the things God has for them. So, if this is you and someone has just tried to speak death over you and told you that you can't fulfill the things God has for you... listen to me they are so wrong.

God is no respecter of person. Your natural age doesn't matter. Look at it this way, imagine the anointing you have on your life now... now imagine it in 10 to 20/30 years. You are going to be so on fire for God.

The ministry God is raising up

in you at this very moment MY GOD!!! That ministry is going to prosper and the people he has for you to minister to!!!! The power behind you being so young and on fire for God is amazing!!! Never let anyone tell you different!!

Be a mighty warrior of God! You're walking with him; you know how good he is and how faithful he is! Keep growing and being all God has called you to be... never turn away!!!

Daily Declarations:

➢ **I will keep pursuing God, I will keep being Obedient, I will not be distracting**

- I will speak life when everyone around me is speaking death
- My anointing will increase, my ministry will prosper, and my life will glorify God

DEMONIC SPIRITS

1 Peter 5:8-9

"Be clear-headed. Keep alert. Your accuser, the devil, is on the prowl like a roaring lion, seeking someone to devour. Resist him, standing firm in the faith."

Sometimes being the only Christian in your household can be difficult. You are able to discern and feel different things in the spirit in which they cannot, you understand things they don't, and you speak in a way they can't.

When you live in that type of household you start to discern different demonic spirits. Those spirits that don't sit right with your spirit. You try to explain it to your family, but they just don't understand that everyone carries spirits whether they are demonic or godly.

If you have a family like mine who allows anyone and everyone to come through the door, then you know how hard it gets to fight these spirits off. You also know how heavy these spirits can weigh on you. You pray and anoint but they are still there, and you don't know what to do.

I've asked myself and God that multiple times. Like God what else is there to do? The burden can be so heavy. There have been times my house didn't feel like home. I hated the atmosphere and the way it made my spirit feel.

However, one night, God told me to just stand firm on his word and he would do the rest. At that point, he revealed the many spirits/demons lingering around my house. He didn't show me them to scare me but so I would stop second guessing myself.

See there are times I think I'm just paranoid and seeing/feeling things, but God always comes in and shows me that I wasn't wrong. SO, what I have to say to you is if you're dealing with spirits lingering around your house ANOINT, PRAY, then STAND FIRM ON THE WORD OF GOD!!! He will come through as he always has and always will!!!

Daily Declarations:

- **Demonic spirits I command you to flee from my household you have no place here!!**
- **I plead the blood of Jesus over my house any spirit not of you Lord I cast down and sent back to the pit of Hell.**
- **I declare that my house is surrounded and protected by God's angelic forces!!**

STEPPING OUT IN FAITH

2 Timothy 1:7

"God didn't give us a spirit that is timid but one that is powerful, loving, and self-controlled."

Sometimes stepping out into faith can be difficult for so many reasons; one is the feeling of being uncomfortable. Believe me, I know. I used to hate to feel uncomfortable.

When I would be asked to pray in front of someone, I wouldn't like it at all because it was uncomfortable. I would be asked to talk in front of people, and I wouldn't like it because it was uncomfortable, and anything else that made me uncomfortable was a fight.

However, as my relationship with God strengthened, I started to learn to step out of my comfort zone. Listen, stepping out of your comfort zone will not only take you to the next level but it will increase your growth in the Lord, your relationship with the Lord, and the blessings from the Lord.

I've learned at such a young age to be ok with being uncomfortable. All you have to do is say, ok Lord I'm not comfortable with what you want me to do but I'm going to step out in faith and be obedient to what you told me to do and as you continue to be obedient when those feelings start to arise, God will use it to Elevate you into your NEXT! God is waiting to see who he can trust.

God gives us so many opportunities and we miss them... don't miss your opportunity! Be comfortable with being uncomfortable!!!

Daily Declarations:

- I will step out of my comfort zone and be obedient to the Lord
- I am a child of the highest King and will rise! The time is now.
- I will not miss my opportunity!

BOLDNESS
Ephesians 3:11-12

"Because of Christ and our faith in him, we can now come boldly and confidently into God's presence.

Today when you hear the word bold you think of someone knowing who they are and entering a conversation knowing that they have the power and access to approach that conversation. You enter it knowing who you are. You enter it believing what you ask will be done. You enter it with confidence.

Well, the same thing goes with God. We are children of the highest king and when we pray, we should be praying boldly. We should enter God's presence with the confidence in knowing I'm the child of the king and I have all authority. We should have God-confidence.

As we enter God's presence boldly, we should see that very thing being done. You should see that ministry prospering, you should see your life blessed, you should see yourself in your dream house, you should see yourself getting the car, SEE IT being done!

In proverbs 18, the word of God tells us there is the power of life and death in the tongue. So, if you know there is either life or death in what you speak wouldn't you rather speak life? There is such a boldness when you speak life over death. When you choose life and not death you make the devil mad.

You see, the devil loves it when we are speaking death... when we choose to speak death it separates us from all the things God has for us but, when we choose life, it births the dreams/visions God has for us!!

Daily Declarations:

- **I will walk boldly and confidently in all the things God has for my life!!**
- **I am a child of the most high king and I will rise!**

- I declare that Gods divine favor is over my life, I am blessed and highly favored!!!

SPIRITUAL RELATIONSHIPS

Proverbs 27:17

"As iron sharpens iron, so one person sharpens another."

As you get saved and start walking this thing out for real, it is critical to surround yourself with Godly people, people that can pour into you, and people who will keep you covered in prayer.

These relationships help you grow in a way you never could have imagined, and not only that, but they are also some of the best relationships you could ever encounter!

In Proverbs, it talks about God's children sharpening one another as iron sharpens iron and it is so critical that you understand that just because your saved does not mean there will not be trials and tribulations. In fact, God tells us there will be trials and tribulations. So, with that being said, we need each other to help pick one another up when the enemy attacks. We need one another to grow in the Lord. We need one another to sharpen each other!!!

If you don't have those Godly friendships, I just encourage you to pray and ask God to have those individuals cross your path. It is so important these relationships empower and push you to be a better you!!

God says ask and you shall receive, so just keep seeking those relationships and stand in faith and trust God! They are coming!!

Daily Declarations:

- ➢ **I will establish Godly relationships**
- ➢ **God will use me to help individuals grow**
- ➢ **I will continue to grow and be the version God has called me to be**

UNANSWERED PRAYERS

Isaiah 40:31

"But those who hope in the Lord will renew their strength. They will soar on wings like an eagle; they will run and not grow weary; they will walk and not faint."

Have you ever felt like you've been faithful and obedient to all God has asked of/from you? You've trusted him? You've given it all to him? After all that, it still seems like your prayers are going unanswered and it just feels like God forgot all about you.

I'm here to tell you that God hasn't

forgotten about you. There is this thing called a waiting period and the amazing thing about the waiting period is the amount of growth and work taking place on the inside of you.

Sometimes God will use the waiting period to test your faith. Are you turning from God because you haven't received what you prayed for? Or are you pressing into God's presence like never before? All these things matter and sometimes you miss the blessings in the waiting because you aren't fully trusting God.

I'm here to tell you that the waiting period will release a strength you never knew you had. When you're in the waiting, we tend to grow weary but with God, you will not!! God will keep you.

The next time you are in the waiting period just remember the greatest work may take place in this season! Keep pressing, keep praying, and keep believing!!! God blesses those who diligently seek him!!!

Daily Devotional:

- ➢ **I will be faithful and obedient even when it feels like you aren't working**
- ➢ **I will seek you in all that I do**
- ➢ **I will trust you no matter my circumstances, you are faithful!!**

DESTINED FOR GREATNESS

YOU ARE QUALIFIED

Jeremiah 29:11

"I know the plans I have for you, plans for good and not evil, plans to prosper and not harm you."

Do you feel like you have nothing to offer? Like you've ruined the plans God has for you? Like you aren't equipped? Well that's the enemy talking, and he is so wrong.

You see the amazing thing about God is his grace and mercy is new each and every day and he is such a forgiving God! You see everything in your past that you feel has disqualified you is erased once you repent and ask for forgiveness!

God created us each with a plan, purpose, and destiny. God created you knowing what you would do and when you would do it before you even did it. God saw all those things and still placed that call on your life because you aren't qualified by this world, but you are qualified by him!!!

The purpose he has for your life is bigger than you could ever even dream. The anointing he's placed on you is stronger than you even know, and the people you are called to touch isn't even imaginable.

God is going to use you in a way you never thought you could be used!! God is getting ready to elevate you and shift you into your next season! A season that is setting you up for the full call and purpose

God has placed on your life.

It is coming SUDDENLY so you better get ready!! A great shift is coming!!! A revival! Those dead things are about to rise, you are about to rise!! Are you ready?

Daily Declaration:

- **I am not disqualified but I am qualified, I am equipped by the king of kings and Lord of Lords!**
- **I speak death unto everything the enemy is trying to place in my mind**
- **I will be ready when God shifts things in my life, I will continue to walk into my purpose**

ABOUT THE AUTHOR

Kalie Klett is a covenant partner at In Faith Ministries International in Lima, Ohio where she is a leader over the children's ministry. She is also part of the Resilient Women's Ministry.

She has been called to help young girls walk boldly and confidently in their purpose and calling. She has also been called to help women who have been abused.

She currently is attending Ohio State Lima for Social Work and plans on continuing until she receives her master's degree. After graduation, she plans on working in a faith-based clinic to help minister to women who have been abused in any way.

She is determined that through the light of Christ women will be redeemed and set free.

www.ingramcontent.com/pod-product-compliance
Lightning Source LLC
Chambersburg PA
CBHW032148040426
42449CB00005B/443